Colliding with God

Other books by Richard Skinner

Leaping & Staggering
(Dilettante 1988/1996)
In The Stillness
(Dilettante 1990)
The Melting Woman
(Blue Button 1993)
Still Staggering
(Dilettante 1995)
Echoes of Eckhart
(Cairns/Arthur James 1998)
The Logic of Whistling
(Cairns 2002)
Invocations
(Wild Goose Publications 2005)
Utterly Staggering
(Wild Goose Publications 2014, download)
A Brief Poetry of Time
(Oversteps 2016)

Colliding with God

New and selected poems
of faith and doubt

Richard Skinner

wild goose
publications www.**ionabooks**.com

© 2017 Richard Skinner

First published 2017 by
Wild Goose Publications, 21 Carlton Court,
Glasgow G5 9JP, UK,
the publishing division of the Iona Community.
Scottish Charity No. SC003794. Limited Company Reg. No. SC096243.

ISBN 978-1-84952-539-8

Cover Image © Petr Strnad. www.youworkforthem.com

Overseas distribution
Australia: Willow Connection Pty Ltd, Unit 4A, 3–9 Kenneth Road,
Manly Vale, NSW 2093
New Zealand: Pleroma, Higginson Street, Otane 4170, Central Hawkes Bay
Canada: Bayard Distribution, 10 Lower Spadina Ave., Suite 400, Toronto,
Ontario M5V 2Z

Printed by Bell & Bain, Thornliebank, Glasgow

Contents

Utterly Staggering:
The story of the first Easter as a lyrical ballad   75

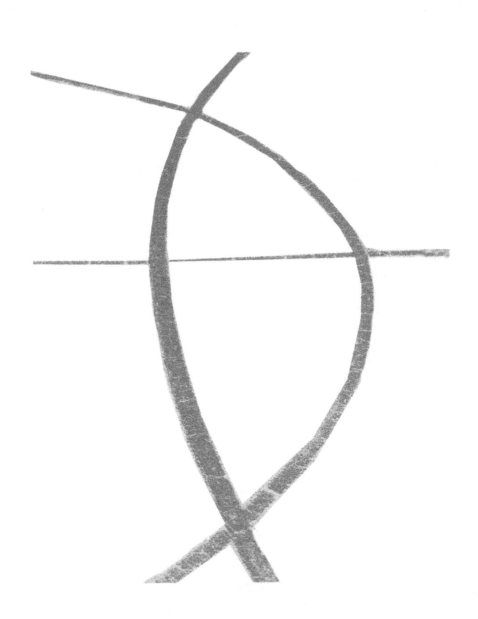

Introduction

The title of this collection is the opening line of the short poem 'Accident' (on page 38), which was written in 1983 and appeared in my first collection *Leaping & Staggering*. In that collection and in later ones there appeared a smattering of other poems which had overtly religious or Christian or spiritual themes, along with three collections which fell exclusively into that category: *In the Stillness, Echoes of Eckhart* and *Invocations*. Given both that some of these collections did not receive a wide distribution and also that I had a number of other such poems yet to be published, I decided to summon the relevant poems from their various haunts to create a religious 'new and selected' collection. This is it. I have, however, not included poems from *Invocations* since it is still easily available from Wild Goose (though a batch of new Invocations is included), nor from *Echoes of Eckhart*, which would have required a long sequence to justify their inclusion. But I have added some poems from my Julian of Norwich sequence, as each is able to stand alone. The collection then concludes with a long poem called *Utterly Staggering*, a retelling of the events of the first Easter as a lyrical ballad.

A few years ago I completed a PhD – nothing to do with poetry, it explored connections between spirituality and evolutionary theory, but I mention it because the nature of the enterprise highlighted by contrast a significant characteristic of putting together a collection of poems: *there is absolutely no need to be consistent from one poem to the next.* Poetry is not simply expressive: it too is a legitimate way in its own right of exploring (to borrow the comic novelist Douglas Adams' expression) 'life, the universe and everything'; but unlike the writing of an academic thesis you are not required to ensure that what you write on page 200 doesn't contradict what you wrote on page 20. No external examiner is going to quiz you along the lines of 'Now, Mr Skinner, in *this* poem you argue such and such, whereas in *that* poem you assert so-and-so. They can't both be right though, can they? Hmm?' – followed by the collapse of the Skinner party. This is lucky – for although in the poems you will probably detect recurring themes (or possibly obsessions), they do not collectively make up any sort of systematic theology. This would be hard – no, impossible – to bring about, since voice is given to such disparate characters and entities as the Tree of the Knowledge of Good and Evil, the Star of Bethlehem, Jesus, a Roman soldier at the crucifixion, St Stephen, and Ananias of Damascus, along with various anonymous narrators, who are not necessarily to be identified as the poet. The lack of an overarching system also means, crucially, that the reader is able to bring his or her own reflections, experiences and understandings to interact, as it were, with the poem, such that the initial act of creation in the making of a poem is complemented and completed by the creativity the reader brings to it by his or her involvement. The creativity is twofold as the poem becomes a joint enterprise. This is your exploration as much as it is mine.

Enough. The poems, not the introduction, are the purpose of the book. Naturally, I hope you enjoy them.

– *Richard Skinner*

Colliding with God

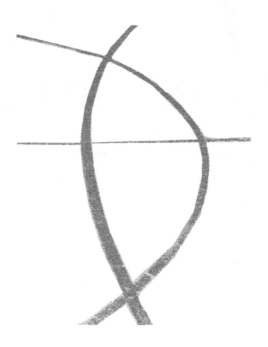

The tree

I was never consulted.
Although central to the whole, giddy,
unfolding drama,
the catalyst without which
neither action nor reaction
could have occurred,
the maypole around which
danced the possibilities
inherent in matter and spirit,
the controlling metaphor
of the narrative ...
I was not consulted.

                    Planted
at the very centre of the garden,
I bore in due season my fruit:
firm, juicy, unblemished, so luscious
as to tempt the Lord God Himself
as he strolled in the cool of the day
through the groves and glades
of His new creation;
for He it was who had planted me,
caused me to flourish and bear fruit;
now He it was who desired to keep
my fruit,
        my luscious fruit,
                    for Himself.

The Lord God had become
a jealous God:
birds were not permitted
to peck my fruit, nor animals
to bite it, nor insects
to bear pollen from flower
to flower – that was a task
only *Ruach* could be trusted with.

When each fruit had ripened,
glowing with maturity,
He gathered all for Himself,
plucking it before it could fall,
before it could decay, before
my seeds could be dispersed.
I would have no descendants;
my fruitfulness would all be
for nothing.

        But there came
the woman, there came
the man, there came
the day when the woman
plucked my fruit,
and the man received it.
The woman and the man,
they bit deep, they devoured
the sweet flesh, with the juice
trickling down their chins;

and the man dribbled
the juice of my fruit
over the breasts
(naked breasts)
of the woman …

She laughed
      as he slowly
            licked it
                  off.

They swallowed the juice,
they swallowed my fruit,
their bodies absorbed it,
my goodness swirled
along their veins,
entered their brains,
became one with their flesh
as their flesh
became one flesh.

And I
    (for one)
        was glad of it.

Being God

Beyond, beneath,
between the God-shot
flux, flow, see –

not randomness,
chaos
unGodded –

see ceaseless creation
creating
Godness,

isness, allness,
ingrained, grained in,
grounded in God;

God, Being, Ground of being
seethes, sustains all being,
Being all, being God.

A little thing

(Julian of Norwich, Revelations of Divine Love, *no.1)*

He placed within my palm a little thing
no larger than a nut, a perfect sphere
on which I gazed with reverential fear.
I asked, 'My Lord, what is this that you bring?'

'It is all that is made,' I heard him say.
'It's all that was, and is, and is to be,
from tiny motes impossible to see,
to every star within the Milky Way.'

I marvelled that it could exist without
directly fading into nothingness,
it was so small a thing. With sweet caress
the answer came, unbound by any doubt:

'It is, because from God its being springs,
whose love creates, sustains and fills all things.'

Song of the star

Am I a comet? Am I a nova?
A planetary conjunction
That's very quickly over?
Am I a fiction, not scientific fact?
Am I immaterial, utterly abstract?
An archetypal image with a psychic function?
Am I simply eye-strain, an optical illusion?
Or maybe the result of a translator's confusion?

Oh no, no, no; I'm none of them:
I am the Star of Bethlehem.

Am I nothing more
Than the arithmetic outcome
Of atoms smashing in my core?
Am I a furnace giving elements their birth?
Or a pretty flower, growing quietly on earth?
Am I on the telly, rich and rather dumb?
Am I just an asterisk, denoting an omission,
Or a footnote afterthought, a textual addition?

Oh no, no, no; I'm none of them:
I am the Star of Bethlehem.

I am a star, shining in my prime;
I am the herald
Of the first Christmas-time;
I am a guide blazing in the sky;
I am the compass point to take your bearings by;
I am reassurance when you are imperilled;
I am a finger, pointing to a stable,
Signalling the downfall of the Tower of Babel.

Ah yes, yes, yes; I'm all of them:
I am the Star of Bethlehem.

I am there

Lift the stone and you will find me,
cleave the wood and I am there;
in the stillness of the water,
in the earth and in the air.

In the light of winter evening
when the trees stretch gaunt and bare,
in the dark when moon is hidden,
I am there, oh I am there.

In the heartbeat, in the bloodstream,
in the muscle, fibre, cell,
I am pulsing, I am quickening …
I am in decay as well:

In the rankness of the garden
unattended, run to seed,
I am dwelling, glorifying
every creature, every weed.

In the cancer, in the warhead,
in the evil, pain, despair,
in the dying, in destruction,
you will find me, I am there.

January 6th

No magi this time,
twelve days late,
lumbering in on camels
with yellow teeth and bad breath,
come to offer strange gifts
to a helpless infant,
along with subtle stellar arts
developed over centuries.

No gold
weighing down the panniers
and wearing holes
in tatty leather pouches;
royal metal fashioned
into bangles, rings, chalices,
and miniature suns
igniting human greed.

No frankincense,
allegedly top quality
(but hard to stop the dealers
cutting it with rubbish);
the ideal smoke
with which to pray to God,
when seeking to persuade,
placate or bribe Him.

No myrrh
in stoppered bottles
made sticky with dribbles;
bitter perfumed gum
to anoint the holy,
sweeten death,
and help the local tarts
enhance their allure.

No, only us,
lounging at the barn door,
discussing politics,
the rising crime rate,
current wars, pollution;
wondering if it's right
to bring another child
into the world.

Gospel psalm

Praise the Lord, my soul!
O Christ, my Lord, how great you are!

You who knew the mysteries of nature,
who knew the goodness of the world;

You looked to the sparrows of the air,
of little account in the trading place,
and saw how not one is forgotten by God;

You watched the ravens feeding, they that neither
sow the seed nor gather harvest,
and saw how God provides for them;

You walked in grassy places, delighting in the wild flowers,
and saw how God has made them all more beautiful
than the finest of fine clothes;

In the fig tree, with its branches growing green and tender,
telling of summer's approach,
you saw the approach of the Kingdom of God;

In the germination of scattered seeds, nurtured by soil,
sprouting by both day and night,
you saw the hidden growth of the Kingdom of God;

In the mustard seed, the smallest of all which grows
to become the largest of plants,
you saw the outspreading of the Kingdom of God;

Flocks of foolish sheep reminded you of other flocks
in need of shepherds of their own;

A clucking mother hen, fussing over her brood of chicks,
touched your spirit and made you weep for Jerusalem;

A simple donkey became your chosen mount
when you entered the city through cheering crowds.

Praise the Lord, my soul!
O Christ, my Lord, how great you are!

Praise the Lord my soul, you who knew
the mysteries of existence,
you who upheld the goodness of life;

You laboured at the carpenter's bench,
and knew the satisfaction of a job well done;

You helped the guests at the wedding feast
enjoy the pleasures of drinking good wine;

You provided five thousand with bread and with fish,
knowing their need to be fed and refreshed;

You took as companions men you could talk with,
share your concerns with, laugh with and be with;

You accepted with gratitude the coolness of oil
and the warmth of the love with which Mary anointed you;

You revealed the presence of God who is with us,
in bread that is broken and wine that is poured,
and life that is shared.

Praise the Lord, my soul!
O Christ, my Lord, how great you are!

Like father, like son

(Julian of Norwich, Revelations of Divine Love, *no.9)*

I saw in Christ what the Father is like
as he spoke of the burden he had borne;
I saw there was only love in his look.

I watched his will subduing the lake
in the turbulent dark before the dawn;
I saw in Christ what the Father is like.

I touched his side when fear seemed to pluck
at my heart and I longed for his concern;
I saw there was only love in his look.

I learned his love makes good any lack
in the love I allow him in return;
I saw in Christ what the Father is like.

I heard his word that they who are bleak
will be blessed and consoled; for all who mourn
I saw there was only love in his look.

I found his grace the key to unlock
and release the delight I cannot earn:
I see in Christ what the Father is like.
I see there is only love in his look.

A tired Messiah looks at his disciples

While watching them, I often think
I did not make the wisest choice.
They're not bad lads, just rather thick:

'Be on your guard against the yeast
of Pharisees,' I warned them once,
meaning: *Beware of false beliefs.*

But they, a bunch of dunderheads,
completely missed the meaning
and thought, *He's noticed we've no bread.*

I sometimes tremble when I think
of what will happen when I leave,
what sort of hash they'll make of things.

But leave I will; I must not ape
the over-anxious parent who
prevents his children growing up;

I must not make decisions which
are theirs to make, or try to live
their lives for them. I'll have to watch

them struggle, fall, get up again,
do many crazy things; and yes,
they'll all be muddled to begin

with, maybe terrified, but they
won't be abandoned to their fate
whatever trials loom – for though

they may be thick, the love of God
can penetrate the thickest. That
is all they'll have, and all they'll need.

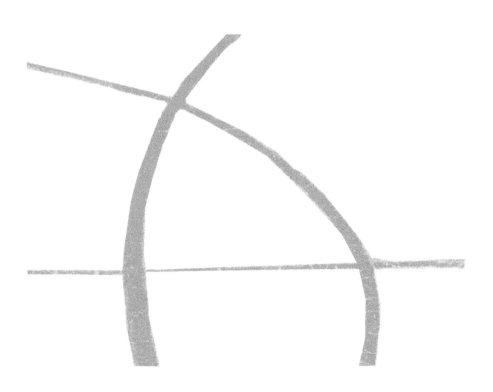

Encounter with Zacchaeus

(Luke 19:1–10)

I saw you up a tree, Zacchaeus,
Saw you up a tree
Peering through the leaves, Zacchaeus,
Peering down at me,
While in the streets of Jericho
The crowd was surging to and fro,
And those who saw you yelled a curse
And called you 'cheat!' or 'scum!' or worse.
With you aloft and me below
I saw your hurt and shame, and so
I called you from your tree, Zacchaeus,
Called you from your tree
To come and talk with me, Zacchaeus,
Talk with me.

I heard them muttering, Zacchaeus,
Heard them muttering
About my choice of friends, Zacchaeus,
While you were stuttering
About the Kingdom and the Way,
And asking me the words to pray
To be forgiven for your sins:
'This is where new life begins;

Repent, believe in God, today
You're free,' was all I had to say
While you were stuttering, Zacchaeus,
You were stuttering,
And they kept muttering, Zacchaeus,
Kept muttering.

But what you did not know, Zacchaeus,
What they did not know,
Is when you climbed that tree, Zacchaeus,
And I was down below,
I felt a shiver and could see
The shadow of another tree,
Another crowd: I heard them curse;
I felt them spit on me and worse.
Ah brother! Brother! Can it be
That you have shown the Way to me?
That through your deeds today, Zacchaeus,
I know the Father's will?
I feel a deathly chill, Zacchaeus,
A deathly chill.

The executioner's tale

I'm the one who hammers in the nails.
Someone has to.
If I refused I'd soon be charged
with insubordination or the like,
and what would happen to the wife and kids
if I lost my job, or worse?

We have a system. The other lads
hold the fellow down, his arms
flat against the cross-piece
(usually he's naked by this time,
all except a bit of cloth
to hide his wedding-tackle. No need
to shock the ladies). Then one of us
must prise his fingers open.

I take a nail (they're about so long)
and hold it upright on the palm.
The hammer is a compact little number:
stubby handle, fairly hefty head,
packs quite a punch. I raise it up,
pause briefly, then sharply bring it down –
thunk! – to drive the nail through hand
and into wood with just one blow.
That at least's the theory. In practice
I have to give more thumps than one.

I ignore the screams (I hear them
but not hear them, as it were);
you have to, drive you crazy otherwise,

and I've long since learned to look away
from the fellow's face. I did look once,
but not a second time. The terror I saw there
made me heave and miss the nail.

We had one bloke who didn't struggle,
didn't scream, didn't even call us
a load of effing b's.
Nice change that. I'm not too sure though
why he said we'd be forgiven since
(to use his words) 'they know not what they do'.
I guess the pain had made him lose his reason,
'cause he was wrong – I know exactly what I do:
I'm the one who hammers in the nails.

In the name

They haunt our history,
echo in our memory:
Aberfan, Lockerbie, Bhopal, Chernobyl.

Each name a distillate of horror
undiluted by the years:
Ypres, Auschwitz, Dresden, Hiroshima.

Each name another entry
in the catalogue of human folly:
Prague, Sharpeville, My Lai, Tiananmen Square.

Each name a fresh wound in the side
where all wounds are the same wound:
Gethsemane, Calvary.

All shall be well

(Julian of Norwich, Revelations of Divine Love, *no.13)*

'"All shall be well"?
How can this be?
When I think of the injury
sin has inflicted
on all your creation,
I cannot conceive
how all shall be well.

'Why is there sin?
Why did you not
prevent us from knowing
the ways of destruction?
All could have been well,
all should have been well
had sin never been.'

'Sin has to be;
but sin will not last,
for the chasm between
your Father and you,
where all that is evil
originates from,
has been closed by my cross.

'By this you may learn
how my powers of healing
surpass every injury
evil can do;

thus all shall be well,
and all shall be well,
and all manner of thing shall be well.'

Reflections of St Stephen

(Acts 6:8–7:60)

Reports of my eloquence
are greatly exaggerated.
I had barely begun to speak
when they bundled me out of the city,
started with the stones.

Each missile that found its target
struck from my lips another word,
as though I were a flint
yielding sparks, which others
since then have fanned into fire.

Mine was a quick death. Many
have been less blessed. Which
is their day? What buildings
commemorate their witness?
Who hereafter will remember them?

Brave for a moment

'There was a disciple in Damascus called Ananias, and he had a vision'
Acts 9:10

What? Him? Coming to Damascus? The news,
Though half-expected, still came as a shock
To everyone here who followed the Way:
That arrogant, fanatical, murderous man
Of Tarsus – the blood of Stephen, our brother,
Staining his hands – had now set his sights on us.

Dreading to think what would happen to us,
We secretly gathered. In the light of this news
Should we flee? Or go underground? A brother
Burst in, out of breath, distraught. Another big shock:
A light in the sky! A voice! The very man
Who threatened us struck blind by God on the way!

We all erupted with relief at the way
In which the living God protected us.
Then came the murmurs of dissent: 'The man
Must think we're mugs,' said one. 'This so-called news
Is meant to make us drop our guard in shock.'
'Heads down and hide,' agreed a second brother.

'But if it's true, then we should call *him* brother,
And visit him,' I ventured. 'That's the way,
Perhaps, to help him through his state of shock?'
'You're mad!' they shouted. 'Are you one of us
Or one of them? We mustn't trust the news;
It's suicide to even see the man.'

That night I could not sleep. A blinded man
In need of help was haunting me. A brother?
I tried to make myself distrust the news,
To no avail. He seemed to be God's way
Of challenging our faith, requiring us
To act upon the gospel, despite the shock.

Brave for a moment, I went. I saw with shock
What God had wrought within this Tarsus man:
Gone was every vestige of his hate for us.
He guessed my doubts, hugged me as a brother,
Prayed for healing, was baptised. Was shown the way
To the synagogue; preached the good news.

Shocking to think of Saul, now Paul, a brother.
Strange man. Forceful. Has to have his own way.
Travels a lot. At times, sends us his news.

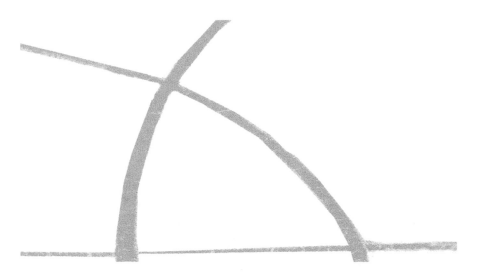

The light of Bede

(c.673–735 AD)

Thirteen hundred years now lie between
His world and ours. Thirteen hundred years
In which the verities of life have been
Repeatedly upturned by pioneers
Of progress, who persistently refuse
To stay within the confines of the given.
They challenge God and brashly break taboos;
Storm the walls of hell in search of heaven.

Or so to Bede it might well seem. To us,
Inheritors of many strands of thought,
The truth of one is not so obvious:
Elusive truth is not so simply caught.
But though beliefs may alter, nothing can
Completely douse the light of Bede the man.

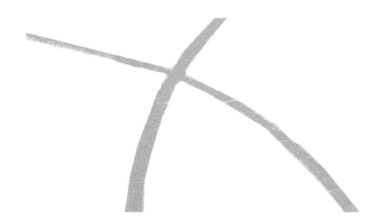

Leaping & staggering

For some,
there is the death-defying leap,
clearing the chasm with one bound,
arms flailing,
a cry of triumph,
all terrors left behind
on the far side,
only joy and happiness
ahead.

For others
(by which I mean you
and me),
there is no triumphal leap,
only a staggering lurch
to the edge of the chasm.
Dizziness strikes,
and a long, sliding, scrabbling descent
is followed
by a long, weary, scrabbling ascent
until, arriving at the top,
we find ourselves, once again,
on the wrong side of the chasm.

And while we staggerers stagger on,
the leapers continue to leap.
One day, perhaps,
we will learn to leap,
and they will learn to stagger.

Accident

Colliding with God,
and wearing no seat-belt,
he suffered extensive injuries
to his life.
They say he is not the same man
since the accident.

God, too, did not escape unscathed,
but received nasty wounds
to his hands and feet,
and a deep laceration in his side.
His condition is said to be critical,
and a full recovery
is unlikely.

Neither party
is covered by insurance.

He will come

I was watching
Mastermind
(and had scored a paltry three)
when He came.

A single
sharp
rap-on-the-door.

Ignoring it,
I answered instead
a question on the Pentateuch.

But got it wrong.

The gods of old

We no longer pray to the bully
swaggering in the playground
while we cower in the toilets
fearing a bloody nose, a twisted arm;

nor to the sarcastic master
whose fine line in humiliation
and outbursts of anger
we anxiously seek to defuse;

nor to Judge Dredd nor to the Terminator
nor to the invading alien nor to any of those
our insecurities could appropriate
to fashion into a fearsome God;

for we are grown-up now, know about
the psychology of projection,
the archetype of the Shadow,
how only fear itself is to be feared:

until, at three o'clock of a sleepless night,
like a river ripping from its channel
in flood, reclaiming its former course,
obliterating our hard-won territory,

the gods of old come rampaging back.

Between

God is in the 'and' of you and me.
Not you, not me; but you and me.

Do not think of a static God:
there is no static God;
only action and reaction,
activity and response,
movement and relationship,
the ceaseless flow
between you and me,
the interplay in which
all cohere.

Do not think of a changeless God:
there is no changeless God.
Without change, there is no movement;
without movement, no relationship;
without relationship, no God.
The only constancy
is the constancy of change;
the moving out of all to all,
the flow and flux between
Blake's flower and star.

Do not think of God beyond
or God within,
but God between;
for in the going between
is the movement of relationship,
and in that movement
there is God.

When God bared his soul

When God bared his soul
we were aghast
and cried out, 'No!
do not burden us
with your troubles!
We have troubles enough
of our own!'

When God bared his soul
we were appalled,
unable to fathom the depths
to which God had sunk;
the despair
which God disclosed.

When God bared his soul
we closed our eyes
and blocked our ears,
trying to hide our own soul
from the ears and eyes
of God.

And God said, 'I will wait
and I will wait, for my troubles
are your troubles; my depths,
your depths; my despair,
your despair. I will wait
and I will wait, for my soul
is your soul; and in the torment
of the waiting, we shall meet.'

Plunge deep

Plunge deep, lunge down into dark,
drop through the soul's dizzy chasm
dismal with unbeing, let spasm
on spasm grip, strip the soul's spark
of all stifling, quenching
self-delusion. Truth is wrenching.

And God labours, craves to birth His Word
anew at centre, enters (is!)
chasm, dark, spark – His
the goad with which the stripped soul is spurred,
the breath by which the spent soul is stirred.

Blizzard

If God were a natural phenomenon
I would nominate blizzard

for its ferocity
embodied in softness;

an obliteration of horizons
into which we are called

like so many Captain Oates
knowing that some time

is an eternity.

Proof

Why do they feel the need
to prove or disprove your existence
with their Unmoved Mover,
First Cause, Ontological Argument;
their convoluted sophistries,
metaphysical disquisitions,
teleological tautologies?

What would they do with irrefutable proof?
How would they respond?
Pray to and praise a philosophical formula?
Be healed by logic?
Or tuck you away in a file
marked QED?

They cannot prove
your existence; but then,
I cannot worship
a proof.

The eighth deadly sin

I have given you, God said, one
for each day of the week – they
will surely suffice – there are
no others.

      But we continued to
importune Him, believing
He had kept the worst for Himself;
until, having shown us His
empty hands in vain, He caused
a deep sleep to engulf us …

               Waking
in the dim light of a new dawn,
we felt a vague sense of guilt
for something the nature of which
still eludes us.

Lent

Give up? Forgo? No! This penitential season
I'll make amends for times-to-laugh unlaughed, lack-
lustre moods, true pleasures unpursued, slack-
hearted days, refusals to rejoice – whatever reason.

I'll unleash my lent-lashed spirit, seize on
each second, beckon forth each soul-spark, crack
wide the wailing-wall within, win back
life, love, laughter, all! Less would be treason!

Let's pretend

Let's play 'let's pretend'.
Let's pretend we care.
Let's act in the way we would act
if we did care.
Let us all become actors
learning our parts –
the words, the gestures:
the nod of the head,
the open arms,
the touch of the fingers
on the small of the back.

Let's play 'let's pretend'.
Let's pretend our vision
is not blurred;
our eyes not deceived
by our own shadows;
let's pretend we see Christ here,
and here, and here,
in those in whom
he is well-hidden.

And undismayed by lines forgotten,
missed rehearsals,
and ineptitude of other actors,
we will not notice as
pretence becomes reality,
vision clarifies,
and what we act
is what we have become.

The sisters and myself

That night and day shall be a single whole
the Sisters pray in ceaseless round. My prayer's
that wind and fire shall both inform my soul.

On starless, moonless nights of darkest kohl
the supplications rise, when man despairs
that night and day shall be a single whole.

When worshipping devoutly, in control
of all my senses – then my spirit swears
that wind and fire shall both inform my soul.

At noon, when I with sun-blind eyes extol
the light, the Sisters kneel. The faith is theirs
that night and day shall be a single whole.

With flesh aroused and Eros on patrol
to heat the blood, I know as passion flares
that wind and fire shall both inform my soul.

At prayer, the Sisters and myself. Our goal
the same, to know the life that life declares:
that night and day shall be a single whole,
that wind and fire shall both inform the soul.

In weal or woe

(Julian of Norwich, Revelations of Divine Love, *no.7)*

Supreme assurance filled my soul. I felt
a peace surpassing all the peace on earth
as though within my heart had ever dwelt
that joy which is the pearl of greatest worth.
A moment later darkness overtook
my senses, all I knew was loneliness,
despair and life's futility. I shook
with fear, uncomforted in my distress.

Again the joy returned, again the pain;
they alternated in my soul until
I saw the lesson of my Lord is this:
that we, in weal or woe alike, remain
within his love, and through it all the will
of God is bringing us to final bliss.

Prayer meeting

The prayer meeting that day
was a quiet affair. No-one
reminded God of His roles
as Creator/Lord/Saviour;

or summarised various sins,
individual and collective,
in terms sufficiently unspecific
to avoid embarrassment;

or gave Him a rundown
of headline news regarding
wars/famines/earthquakes/
abductions/elections/plane crashes;

or advised Him of forthcoming events
for which fine weather/money/
good attendance/more volunteers
would be highly desirable;

or explained to Him that people suffering
from sickness/diseases/broken limbs/
unhappiness (with named examples)
were all in need of healing …

Instead, we entered a silence
beyond all words,
a silence that deepened
and thickened like honey in winter.

Meditation on peace

Peace is not a thing to possess
> but a way of possessing;

Peace is not a gift to be given,
> but a way of giving;

Peace is not a topic to teach,
> but a way of teaching;

Peace is not a theory to learn,
> but a way of learning;

Peace is not an opinion to hold,
> but a way of holding;

Peace is not a resolution of strife,
> but a way of striving;

Peace is not a creed to preach,
> but a way of preaching;

Peace is not a God to serve,
> but a way of serving;

Peace is not a question to ask,
> but a way of asking;

Peace is not an answer to seek,
> but a way of seeking;

Peace is not a journey's end,
> but a way of journeying.

Stale bread

the bread
was stale;
    and I wonder
    was your body
    stale?

the wine
was Sainsbury's best;
    and I wonder
    was your blood
    Sainsbury's best?

no neat equations,
no analytic laws,
identify
    stale bread
    and Sainsbury's best
    with body
    and with blood.

no statute of the state,
no rule of thumb,
can justify
    the logic
    of the altar rail.

and yet … and yet
the wisdom of the intellect,
when at the rail, must confess
the splendid ordinariness
    of stale bread
    and Sainsbury's best.

Bread is broken

Bread is broken, wine is poured
In remembrance of the Lord
Who has called us all to be
As open to our God as he.

Not in careless solitude
Is a life with God pursued,
But immersed within the ways
By which his world lives out its days.

Loves and doubts, and hopes and fears
Make the pattern of our years;
Which with every passing week
Is where we'll find the God we seek.

Casting shadows

(Julian of Norwich, Revelations of Divine Love, *no.14)*

I saw this truth: the wrath that we perceive
to be of God lies in ourselves alone,
a shadow which we cast (and then disown)
upon our Lord. In error we believe

that he has cast a shadow over us
of judgement, condemnation, suffering
for every failure, sin and evil thing
we think we're guilty of. Never thus

our Lord! His goodness, truth and love, his power
and peace preclude all anger; and between
our soul and him no wrath can intervene,
however dark or dreadful be the hour.

Fragments of epiphany

Bedazzlement
upon Damascus roads
cannot be guaranteed.

Phenomena
of comet and eclipse
can be misread.

> Descending doves
> and tongues of fire,
> mystic visions
> of the heavenly choir,
> a night-time voice,
> a miracle wrought:
>> unmistakable signs,
>> but given, not bought.

Epiphanies
lurk under stones
and in the trees,

abiding in
(dependent on)
the commonplace:

the sight
of a heron's
lazy flight,
the cry
of a buzzard
circling high,
a constellation recognised,
a wild flower named:
        fragments of epiphany
        waiting to be claimed.

Today, out walking

Today, out walking,
I opened my eyes and created
a flock of lapwings, glittering
like moonlight on the sea.

Today, out walking,
I opened my eyes and created
a river, deep and dark and smooth,
like polished ebony.

Today, out walking,
I opened my eyes and created
an alder, an ash and a beech;

I opened my eyes and created
bullocks in a field,
herb Robert in a hedgerow,
an oil beetle on a blade of grass;

I created a gibbous moon,
two new constellations,
the entire Milky Way.

One day, out walking,
I will open my eyes and create
God.

The wisdom of trees

The wisdom of trees
is drawn from the roots,
distilled in the sap,
hidden in the hardness.

The wisdom of man
is drawn from his depths,
distilled in his thoughts,
hidden in his heart.

The wisdom of God
is drawn from the Father,
distilled in the Spirit,
manifest in the Son.

Seams

We have been
working this seam for too long;
the quality of what we extract
has markedly diminished;
it neither feeds the fires
of our imagination nor quickens
the heart.

We have heard of
other seams, loaded (it is said)
with ore as rich in the spirit
as any we have found, plunging
as deep (some would say deeper)
into the rock. Tempting
to try one.

We, however,
have been shaped by this seam,
are accustomed to its vagaries;
another seam would not be
our seam, would not accommodate
our contours; could well resist
the tools we have fashioned
over the centuries.

We resume
our tunnelling into the dark,
now with the suspicion it is we,
all along, who are the seam
being worked.

Probes

My first, a christening present,
transmits on a single, fundamental
frequency. Although the clarity astonishes,
the content never varies and I
have long since stopped tuning in.
The transmissions continue nonetheless.

My second, which I launched
in my twenties, hurtles along
an unplottable course, liberally
transmitting on all possible frequencies:
a marvellous cacophony which
I am still hoping to translate.

Transmissions from my third,
dispatched ten years ago, mystically
consist of sporadic static punctuated
by fragments of apparent lucidity.
It is the periods of silence, however,
which make the most sense.

The fourth, launch-date unknown,
will dispense with all transmissions. Being
the last in the series, it will be manned.

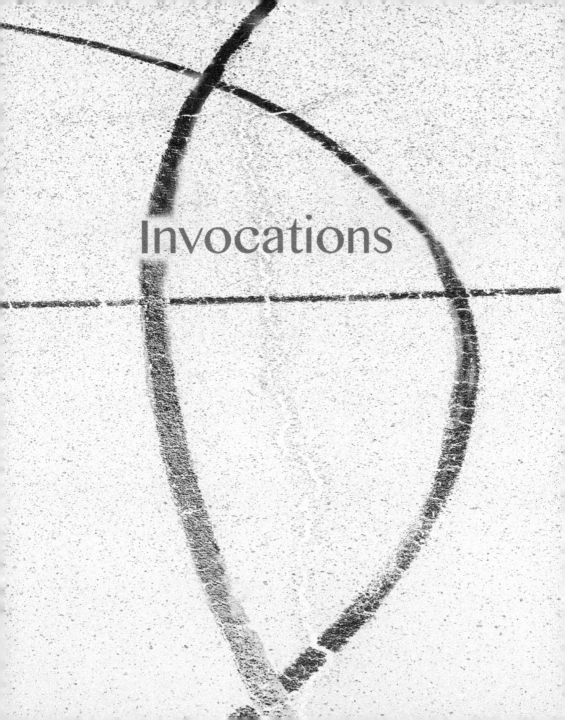

Invocations

O Snow Goose
winging your way across the sky,
spanning land and sea,
free as the air that bears you,
sounding your signature clarion call;
you are a denizen of heaven:
come, awaken us with each wing-beat,
call us to follow in freedom's way.

O Dove
cooing in the quiet evening,
softness concealing strength,
renowned as the bearer of the olive leaf
back to the ark;
you are the icon of peace:
come, quieten the clamour of our lives,
strengthen our soft resolve.

O Triplet of Hares
circle-dancing in a sunlit field,
boxing bouts with mates and rivals,
not the madness of tradition
but exuberance in the springtime of the year;
you are the overflow of life's energy:
come, embrace us in your threefold unity,
overfill us with your exuberance.

O Fern

ancient life inhabiting the many terrains
of mountain and desert, woodland and moor,
emerging in the warmth of spring,
fronds unfurling to capture the sunlight:
you are nature's interrogative:
come, inhabit the terrain of our soul,
enlighten us with your questions.

O Fishes
darting among the weeds,
gliding between the riverbed pebbles,
dependent on the fresh replenishment
of the life-giving current;
you are the glimpse beneath the surface:
come, refresh our imagination,
entice us into the stream of life.

O Salmon
leaping with life in your natal stream,
contending with the contrary current,
returning to your origins
to bring forth the next generation;
you are the triumph against the odds:
come, endow us with your persistence,
return us to our true origins.

O Lagoon
haven from the roaring surf,
where the shoreline shrubs scatter their leaves
and your welcoming waters are tinctured
with healing essence;
you are balm for the body and salve for the spirit:
come, entice us with your tincture,
that we may bathe in your benediction.

O Whisper
messenger of murmured words
skimming like a skater along the edge of hearing;
tantaliser of the attentive ear
with your subtle undertones and hushed utterances;
you are the transmitter of secrets:
come, entrust to us
the life-giving secret our souls crave.

O Touch
consoling with a hand on the shoulder,
arousing with lips on the breast,
healing with fingers of a stranger,
caring with a bear-hug from a friend;
you are affirmation, you are belonging:
come, reach us through the simple gesture,
dispel our pain of isolation.

O Breath
unregarded rhythm of the day,
unremitting guardian of the night,
whose presence is a silent working in the blood,
whose absence is an anguished gasp;
you are instinct, you are necessity:
come, enter us, do not withhold yourself,
moment by moment inspire us.

O Flesh
electrifying and sorrowful,
echoing the world in optic nerve and fingertip;
desiring, desirous, importunate and wayward,
spirit written in a double helix;
you are us, we are formed of you:
come, echo through our every synapse,
importune us with your every desire.

O Riverhead
known to stonechat and lark
on the high moor,
seepage of pellucid water pure and cool,
and promise of a distant sea;
you are our destination across the heather and granite:
come, let us drink of you,
the source of all refreshment.

O Abba
dancing with the queen of heaven,
responding to our soul's SOS,
knowing me by name;
but does your mother know
you are the Super Trouper?
come, take a chance on me,
bring me to my Waterloo.

Utterly Staggering
The story of the first Easter as a lyrical ballad

Introduction

This poem may well irritate biblical scholars, ignoring as it does various differences among the four Gospels, such as the timing of the Last Supper – was it a Passover meal (celebrating the release of the Hebrew people from captivity in Egypt centuries earlier), as Matthew, Mark and Luke claim, or did it take place the evening before Passover, as John recounts it? And which of Jesus' followers are supposed to have discovered the empty tomb? Were the discoverers confronted by one angel or two? Or were they young men? Again, the gospels differ.

I ignore these problems. I am not 'doing history', nor even really 'doing theology', even though certain theological presuppositions are inevitably implied (in, for example, having Jesus refer to himself as 'a mere man'). What I am doing is taking elements of a story which, though very familiar to many people, is unfamiliar, or familiar in fragmentary fashion, to many others, and narrating it in a manner that I find appealing and accessible. Maybe others will too.

The principal verse form is the quatrain, with three stresses in each line. Occasional lines have four or two stresses, and some stanzas have six lines. These variations being inspired by Coleridge's 'The Rime of the Ancient Mariner', the poem belongs to the 'lyrical ballad' tradition.

1. The Last Supper

That time of the year had arrived
When every Jew celebrates,
So Jesus went up to Jerusalem
Along with a number of mates.

He'd arranged for a room to be ready
Where they could meet for a meal;
The food was inviting, the flagons were full:
No hint of a coming ordeal.

The feasting was well under way
When Jesus sprang his surprise.
He tapped on the table for silence:
'Hey, listen to me, you guys;

'I haven't had time to tell you
All that I hoped I would –
You'll have to think for yourselves from now on.'
But none of them understood.

'It's one of his stories!' said Peter,
'Admittedly somewhat obscure.'
The others were nodding agreement,
'Cept Thomas, who wasn't so sure.

(For Thomas the Twin was a sceptic
Known to take nothing on trust.
Irrefutable proof was his watchword,
And doubt was an absolute must.)

'I'm going to leave you,' said Jesus,
Taking and breaking the bread.
'To put it more bluntly,' he splashed out the wine,
'This time tomorrow – I'm dead.'

'Poppycock!' Peter protested,
'We don't want defeatism here!
The lads and I are ready and willing
To get out there and do some killing –
It's Roman blood that we'll be spilling!'
The others let loose a loud cheer.

'Hold on to your horses,' said Jesus,
'That wouldn't be any good:
Son of Man's gotta do what Son of Man's gotta do …'
Still none of them understood.

'It's the moment of truth,' he continued,
'In doing the Father's will.
Blood'll be spilt, I admit it,
But mine, on Golgotha Hill.'

'We'll never desert you,' cried Peter
Giving a twirl of his sword,
'Depend on us, Jesus – nothing could please us
More than defending our Lord!'

But smiling the faintest of smiles,
Jesus said, 'Don't be a clot;
Before the cock crows in the morning
You'll claim not to know me three times on the trot.'
I'll show him, thought Peter, subsiding,
Whether he likes it or not.

Now Judas was sitting at table,
Judas who managed the cash.
He'd hatched up a plan with the High Priest
(For Judas was brainy and brash).

The plan was quite simple: he'd promised
To hand over Jesus that night
For the sake of a handful of silver –
A nice little earner all right.

None of the others had guessed it
Though Jesus had worked out the score:
'Judas,' he said, 'aren't you going
To … er … offer a gift to the poor?'

Judas was taken aback
And almost resolved to sit tight;
But his soul had been snared, so he slipped
Silently into the night.

2. The arrest of Jesus

The meal was over. Said Jesus,
'Let's get some fresh air, my lads!'
So they went for a stroll in the garden
Where Jesus felt tired and sad.

With Jimmy and Johnny and Peter
He wandered on further ahead.
He begged of them, 'Wait here on watch,
'Cause this is the moment I dread.'

Another few yards on his own
Before he sat under a tree
And frantically launched into praying,
'Father, O Father, it's me:

'The future is feeling quite scary;
I'm frightened I've got it all wrong.
Are you sure that the plan
Is for me, a mere man,
To carry the can?
Quite frankly, I'm not all that strong.'
But he knew as he prayed that the answer
Was there in his heart all along.

He opened his eyes. 'Hey, fellows!
It's time to get going,' he said.
But Jimmy and Johnny were snoring,
And Peter looked three-quarters dead.

He shook them awake (rather roughly),
And called them a right dozy crew
As they shambled along to the others
Who hadn't a clue what to do;

For suddenly out of the gloom
A menacing crowd had appeared
Which Judas was leading to Jesus.
Said Peter, 'It's just as I feared!

'That 'orrible toe-rag has tricked us –
I'm now gonna give 'im what-for!'
Stopping him Jesus said, 'Peter!
Remember that love is God's law.'
To Judas he added, 'My brother!
I'll kiss you in friendship once more.'

A bit of a barney erupted
And one of the crowd lost his ear;
With a swish of a sword it was severed,
But Jesus said, 'Don't interfere!

'The workings of God are unfolding
As scripture has warned us they would.'
As he healed the ear of the fellow,
His disciples all scarpered as quick as they could.

3. Jesus before the Council

Now Caiaphas the High Priest had called
The Council to meet at his house.
'We've got him! And now we can squash him
As though we were squashing a louse!

'Bring the man in, let him try
To answer the blasphemy charge
Of claiming to be the Messiah
Wandering around at large.'

Jesus was brought in before them.
He listened in dignified silence,
Aware that the witnesses called to denounce him
Had been nobbled to gain their compliance.

'He healed a man on the Sabbath
By calling on Satan,' they said.
'And he claimed he could topple the temple
And raise up a new one instead.'

The witnesses' lies were a mishmash,
Their evidence riddled with gaps;
The Council was fuming and starting to flap:
Would the case against Jesus collapse?

Peter, meanwhile, had come sneaking
Into the courtyard outside,
Hoping to hear what was happening
While looking for somewhere to hide.

But the night air was bitterly cold,
And a fire seducingly hot …
Temptation was strong and he couldn't resist
The lure of a comfortable spot.

'Hello handsome!' a servant-girl giggled,
Lingering close to his place.
'You look cosy! You fancy a cuddle?'
He furtively shaded his face.

'Here,' said the girl looking closer,
'You're with that Jesus, you are!'
'No I'm not! Go away!' Peter snapped.
'Charming!' she said. 'You'll go far!'

She went to her friends and confided:
'See the geezer what's sat over there?
You can tell by his voice where he comes from,
Same place as that Jesus, I'd swear.'
'Don't listen to her, she's a liar!'
Bawled Peter the length of the square.

Still silent in front of the Council
Jesus could hear Peter's yell,
And though he had known his friend would disown
Him, it hurt him, it hurt him like hell.

So when the High Priest thumped the table
And shouted, 'Enough of this play!
You claim you're the Christ, is that so?'
Jesus just shrugged, 'As you say.'

'We've got you!' the Council exulted,
Doing high-fives all around.
'It's Pilate for you, mister wise-guy,
Then the cross and the burial ground!'
They spat in his face and they slapped him,
Delighted they'd finally trapped him.

Peter, outside, was still warming
His hands and his feet by the fire,
When others came up and accused him:
'You say that that girl is a liar,

'But surely she has to be right –
You're one of the Galilee men;
You've been with that Jesus for years!'
But Peter denied it again.

'Absolute bunkum!' he blustered.
'Others might call him their Lord,
But I've never favoured the fellow;
I know for a fact he's a fraud.'

Dawn was approaching, and Jesus
Was led from the room where he'd been;
They took him outside to the courtyard
Where Peter was still to be seen.

The sound of a cockerel crowing
Made Peter look up with a start;
Jesus nearby had a look in his eye
That stabbed at him right in the heart.
You'll claim not to know me three times …
Stabbed at him right in the heart.

4. Jesus before Pilate

Jesus was taken to Pilate,
The Governor over Judaea
Who devoted his life to exploring
Ways to advance his career.

'Why have you brought him before me?'
He wearily asked the Chief Priest.
'What crime do you claim he's committed?
And make it half-likely at least.'

'He says he's the King of the Jews;
That's blasphemy, so he must die!'
'Don't make me laugh,' grunted Pilate.
'I'm going to release him. Goodbye!'

'Release him? With greatest respect
We beg of you, sire, don't try it.
This ruffian's an out-an-out nutter!
He'll stir up one hell of a riot.'

A riot, thought Pilate, oh great,
Why does it happen to me?
A riot's the last thing I want
To be putting down on my C.V.

'Well, you,' he glared in annoyance,
'Out with it then, what's your game?'
'To tell of God's truth,' Jesus answered,
'Truth is the reason I came.'
'Don't give me that! What is truth?'
Pilate was quick to exclaim.

This is a nonsense, he pondered,
But thanks to these lunatics
It looks like I'll have to rely on
The Department of Dirty Tricks.

'Today is a day,' he announced,
'When one of the prisoners goes free;
The plebs and the proles can decide
Precisely which one that'll be:

'Jesus the so-called Messiah,
Or Barabbas we-all-know's a thief.
It's this chap they'll want handed back,
That's my official belief.'

The crowd soon amassed and was chanting,
Sounding in vigorous voice.
Pilate stepped forward: 'Barabbas?
Or Jesus? It's wholly your choice.'

'Barabbas!' they shouted. 'Barabbas! Barabbas!
Give us Barabbas! We want him set free!
Barabbas! Barabbas! Barabbas! Barabbas!
Give us Barabbas we want him set free!
Barabbas! Barabbas! Just gives us Barabbas!
Barabbas! Barabbas! We want him set free!'

Pilate didn't realise
The seething, surging mob
Had cleverly been worked on
By those who knew their job.

'It's Barabbas you're wanting released,
You're sure of it now?' he said.
'If you want my opinion, I reckon
You've collectively gone off your head.

'And what do I do about this one?
You're saying you want him to die?'
And the mob bellowed out in a fury,
'Crucify! Crucify! Crucify!'

'Water!' snapped Pilate. 'To wash with,
So everyone here understands
I've done what I can for the fellow.
I don't want his blood on my hands.'

5. The Crucifixion

Jesus was dragged off by soldiers
Who made him the butt of their jokes;
They stripped him and whipped him and beat him,
Then put round his shoulders a cloak.

And one plucked a strand from a thorn-bush
And twisted it round and around
To fashion a circle of skin-tearing barbs
That they rammed on his head as a crown.

'O King of the Jews!' they acclaimed him
And mockingly started to bow,
'O mightiest ruler, pray tell us
Where is your "kingdom" right now?'

Now Jesus felt mightily battered,
And Jesus felt bleakly alone;
He thought of what still lay before him
And uttered a terrible groan.

'None of that nonsense, you jerk!
We're Romans, we don't give a toss!
And it's time to get going, look lively …
Oi you! You're forgetting your cross!'

As they heaved it onto his shoulders
He tried very hard not to flinch,
And summoning up the dregs of his strength
He dragged it barely an inch;
So they lashed him and thrashed him anew,
But he dragged it barely an inch.

They brought in a bystander, Simon,
To carry the cross up the hill
(Known in the region as Golgotha
Or 'Place of the Skull') until
They called a halt at the top
Where Simon could let the thing drop.

Two other prisoners were present
Sentenced to death for the crime
Of robbing and beating up travellers.
A soldier was laughing: 'This time
It's a couple of crooks and a king!'
As the hammers were starting to swing.

Soon they had hammered the nails
Through both of his hands and his feet,
Then hauling the crucifix upright
Their authorised task was complete.
They lounged about uttering oaths
As they idly diced for his clothes.

Jesus, above them, was sweating;
The heat of the day grew intense;
The welts from the whips were a torment;
The strain on his arms was immense.
Then sightseers had to arrive
To argue how long he'd survive.

6. The disciples and the women

All of this time the disciples,
Who'd slung their hooks,
Were skulking around the city
Like a bunch of crooks,

Anxious to hear what rumours
Were being spread,
But far more anxious not
To end up dead.

And hearing the shouts of the mob
Loud and clear,
They scuttled away to their room
Gripped by fear.

Then news came along that Judas
Had done himself in.
'God rot him, the scumbag,' said one
With a ghastly grin.

'Well, yes,' another said slowly,
'The trouble is, chaps,
We haven't behaved much better.
Worse, perhaps:

'Boasting how loyal we were
In front of the Master,
Then running away like girlies …
We're a disaster!

'I say we should rally around,
Show him we care.
Why don't we go up to Golgotha?
Be with him there?'

They agreed, and the absence of anyone
After them meant
A miraculous comeback of courage.
They upped and went.

It was humbling to get there and find
The 'girlies' already
Were gathered and keeping a vigil:
Unswervingly steady.

Scorning the soldiers' mockery
They'd all agreed
They wouldn't abandon Jesus
In his hour of need;

So here they were, watching and weeping,
Alongside their friend,
Praying and praying and praying
His torment would end.

One of their number was Mary
Whose life had been
A hideous mess until Jesus
Had intervened.

He'd hauled out the horrors inside her
And sent them packing;
Bestowing on her in their place
The love she'd been lacking;

Love which had brought her alive
These past two years,
Love which could show itself now
Only in tears.

The women, they welcomed the men.
Together they stood,
Numbed at the sight of the figure
On his cross of wood.

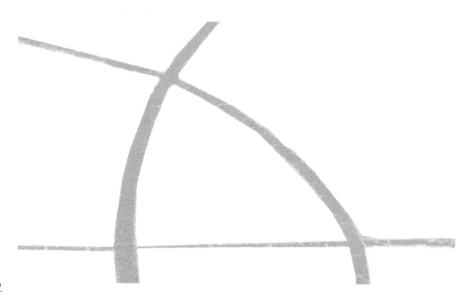

7. The death of Jesus

Jesus could barely see:
'Johnny – that you standing there?
Look after my mother from now on,
Take her into your care.

'And ma – take Johnny's advice,
He'll know what to do for the best.
I know it must hurt you, me being like this ...'
He could not utter the rest.

Exhausted, he let his eyes close
Wondering, how much more?
And what of all those who had trapped and betrayed him,
How could he even the score?

'Forgive them!' he managed to mutter
Though one pain followed another;
'Father, forgive them! Reclaim them!
I love them – I am their brother.'

The crowd now began
Jeering and booing:
'Hey, Son of Man!
This ain't the behaviour
We want from a Saviour!
Come down from the cross,
See if you can!

What? Nothing doing?
You're a dead loss!'

'Hey, Mr Messiah!'
(They carried on booing)
'Summon down fire!
Or call up an angel –
The heavenly choir!
Show us a miracle,
Something empirical!
Still nothing doing?
You're a cheat and a liar!'

One of the robbers beside him
Started to jeer at him too:
'If you're what it means to be holy
Then stuff it – stuff God and stuff you.
You're dying like us, have you got it?
And there's nothing at all you can do!'

'Shut it, you fool,' said the other,
'The guy's in a terrible state.
Though we've had it coming for ages
He doesn't deserve this fate …
When you enter the kingdom,' he added to Jesus,
'I hope you'll remember me, mate.'

'Thank you, my friend.
We will meet again.
In paradise, friend,

In paradise, when
All will be healed,
All be revealed.'

Darkness descended over the land
Although it was noon;
For three more long hours Jesus hung there,
Half in a swoon.

Words from the scriptures kept flickering
Through his consciousness:
The law and the prophets, the wisdom, the psalms;
God's promises.

But where was the Father, where had He gone?
He wasn't there:
And Jesus cried out from the depths of his soul
In sudden despair,
'My God! You have left me! Why leave me, my God?'
His final prayer.

'He's saying he's thirsty,' said someone. 'His mouth
Is all full of gunge.'
So they held to his lips for him to sip
A wine-soaked sponge.

But the ordeal of Jesus was over,
For he was dead;
And the crown of thorns, it still adorned
His bloodied head.

The watching crowd fell silent,
Suddenly ashamed;
Then piercing the silence the voice
Of a soldier exclaimed,
'He was the Son of God all right,
As his followers claimed.'

And the curtain tore in the temple
With a terrible sound.
No more would the Holy of Holies be
Out of bounds;
The sacred and profane are both
Holy ground.

8. The burial of Jesus

The Council went off to find Pilate.
'Not you lot again,' he sighed;
'Haven't you done enough mischief for now?
The fellow's been crucified.'

'We do have another request:
Tomorrow's the Sabbath, you see;
And crucified bodies remaining on view
Are a terrible blasphemy.'

'Oh very well, I'll have him removed
Along with the other two.
The soldiers'll see to it later today;
Now please, I've got masses to do –

'And don't get ideas; I've just told
Some loser called Joseph that he
Can dispose of the body – he seemed pretty keen,
Though why he should want it beats me.'

Alarmed by the new information
The Council quickly conferred:
Suppose his disciples make off with the body
After it's been interred?

A devious bunch, they would claim
The man had come back from the dead …
'Er, may we suggest a guard on the tomb?
Just a precaution,' they said,

'To nip in the bud any plan
For disruption they might be devising,
With hooligans, yobbos and general riffraff:
Nobody wants an uprising.'

Later that day the soldiers returned
To check up that Jesus had died;
A task they got through in a second or two
By shoving a sword in his side.

Water and blood both oozed from the wound,
Splashed on the earth below;
And the sun-baked soil did not recoil
From the lifeless crimson flow.

Then Joseph from Arimathea arrived
To take down the corpse from the cross;
He carried it through to a garden tomb
Where he laid it, in linen, on moss.

A boulder was sweatingly rolled up in front,
And soldiers were ordered to stay:
All this to ensure that nothing could conjure
The body of Jesus away.

Now Mary was there in the garden,
Watching with grief in her heart,
Wanting to be with her healer and teacher,
Wanting to play her part.

As his body had not been anointed
She resolved when the Sabbath was past
To return with a mixture of perfume and spices
To honour her friend to the last.

9. The empty tomb

The Sabbath was over, and Peter
Was feeling extremely depressed.
'Anyone any suggestions
What we should do for the best?'

None of the others responded,
Except with a shrug or a snort;
Unable to muster between them
A solitary sensible thought.

And there they would surely have stayed
Stewing away in their gloom
Had a whirlwind not whirled in and spun them around
As Mary dashed into the room:
'He's not … No! It's not … No! There's not …
I mean – empty – it's empty – the tomb!'

'What are you on about, Mary?'
Johnny grabbed hold of her arm.
'You're making a fool of yourself:
Can't you try, just for once, to be calm?'

'We went to anoint him,' she panted,
Nervously tugging her hair,
'But somebody's managed to open the tomb,
And the Master – his body's not there!'

Most of the men tapped their temples:
'Come off it – you've got to be wrong!
You're just a hysterical woman!

Admit it, you're having us on!'
But Peter and Johnny together
Had dived for the door and were gone.

They dashed down the road in a frenzy
Barging through crowds on the way,
And reaching the tomb in the garden
Johnny cried out in dismay;

For Mary was right, and the stone
That should have been sealing the tomb
Was rolled to one side of the entrance.
Pausing, he peered in the gloom.

But a pumped-up and passionate Peter
Impatiently pushed him away,
Went blundering in to see for himself
Where surely his dead Lord still lay.

The linen was all he could find
Neatly laid out on the ground;
The linen and nothing much else:
The shock was abrupt and profound.

'It's crazy!' he spluttered. 'It's madness!
What's going on? This is weird!
His body was put here by Joseph,
How can it have just disappeared?'

Then Johnny came into the tomb.
'It's happened,' he soberly said.
'Think of those hints he kept dropping:
I reckon he's no longer dead.'

10. Jesus appears to Mary Magdalene

As Peter and Johnny returned,
Disputing what could have occurred,
Mary came back to the garden
Refusing to be deterred.

She wept as she thought of her Lord
Murdered by unfeeling men;
She wept as she thought she would never
Set eyes on her teacher again;
She wept as she thought of a future
With no-one to love and to tend.

A figure was standing nearby
Who asked her, 'Why are you crying?'
The gardener, she thought. He might know
Where the body of Jesus is lying.

'Oh tell me, sir, please will you tell me
Where you have taken him to?
Where is my Lord? Won't you tell me?
Please help me – oh, what should I do?'

Still weeping, she begged him again
And again to let her know where he
Had taken the body of Jesus …
Then the voice she adored answered, 'Mary!'

She clapped both her hands to her mouth:
It isn't the gardener! It's him!
He's alive! But how can that be?
She swayed … her eyesight went dim.

She grabbed hold of Jesus and held him.
'Hey careful! You'll squeeze me to death!'
He smiled and released her. 'Now, Mary,
Let me re-gather my breath!

'There's a couple of things I must tell you:
To start with, I really am grateful
For all you have done, and especially
The wonderful way you've stayed faithful.

'Now secondly, run to the others
And give them this message from me:
We're going to meet up together again,
Jerusalem first, and then by the sea.

'And, Mary, I will soon return
To the Father – my Father and yours;
But don't be afraid of the future,
Everything's part of God's cause.'

Bursting with joy, she departed
To do as he'd asked there and then;
The disciples were stunned to be told
The Lord was alive once again,
And he had appeared to a woman
Before he'd appeared to the men.

11. Jesus appears to the men

Later on, when it was dark,
Two weary travellers burst in:
'You'll never believe what has happened,
It's sent us both into a spin.

'We were well on the way to our village
When this stranger appeared out the blue.
He asked us a shed-load of questions
Then claimed it's the scriptures come true!

'We had to hear more, so we asked him
To share in our food – just some bread:
He took it, and broke it – just amazing!
It was Jesus! Come back from the dead!'

The disciples were still in an uproar
When into the room stepped the proof.
'Evening all,' Jesus said. 'How's it going?'
And they practically shot through the roof.

'How'd you get into the room?'
Cried Peter like someone accursed.
'Through the door,' said the Lord, and Peter exclaimed,
'It's usual to open it first!'

'Now calm yourselves down,' said Jesus,
'I'm here to let you all know
That though I am only around for a while
You won't be alone when I go.

'You'll be filled with the Spirit of God
Who will … how can I put this? Inspire
You such that my gospel – are you taking this in? –
Will spread through the world like a fire.'

For reasons best known to himself
Thomas the Twin wasn't there.
But when he turned up, and the others
Excitedly started to share
The utterly staggering news,
Thomas said simply, 'Oh yeah?'

They couldn't begin to convince him
No matter how often they tried;
Till Jesus returned and revealed
The wounds in his hands and his side:
'At last! Irrefutable proof!
My Lord and my God!' Thomas cried.

'So seeing, for you, is believing,'
Jesus told Thomas, 'but they
Whose belief is a seeing within
Are doubly happy, I'd say.
And faith will be seeing tomorrow
What you have been seeing today.'

12. A lakeside encounter

The final appearance of Jesus
Happened in Galilee.
The disciples had suffered a miserable night
Unsuccessfully fishing the sea.

He stood on the shoreline and shouted:
'What have you caught then, you guys?'
'Not a thing! Not a bean! Not a sausage!'
Was the gist of their replies.

'Well, try to the right over there,
I can see quite a sizable school!'
So they tried to the right as suggested
And netted a whopping great haul.

'It's Jesus!' said Johnny. 'No wonder
He knew where the fish would be lurking.
Hey, Peter! Where are you going!
This is no time to be shirking!'

For Peter had leaped overboard
And was sloshing his way to the land,
Leaving the other disciples
To pull up the boat on the sand.

'Well, Peter,' said Jesus, 'you hungry?
I'm cooking some breakfast, okay?
Some bread and some fish, like the old times.
But first, I've got something to say:

'You love me, old friend, am I right?'
'You know that I do!' Peter cried.

'Then continue my work with the lonely and lost
As companion, protector and guide.

'You love me, old friend?' he repeated.
'You know that I do!' Peter cried.
'Then continue my work with the seekers of truth,
And enlighten the mystified.

'You love me, old friend?' for a third time.
'You know that I do!' Peter cried.
'Then continue my work for the rest of your life,
Spreading my gospel worldwide.'

How many more times? thought Peter,
Beginning to feel aggrieved.
And why do I get the impression
I'm not actually being believed?

Three times on the trot he's now asked me …
Three times! You moron, of course!
He knows ever since I denied him three times
I've suffered appalling remorse.

He's telling me how he still trusts me,
Which means that the past is the past!
Thank God, it means that me and the others
Can get on with the future, at last!

A load had been lifted; his life
Would no longer be burdened with dread.
The others now joined them, and Peter
Passed round the fresh broken bread.

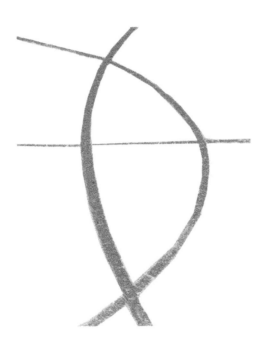

Notes

'I am there': the first two lines are words attributed to Christ in the text known as the Gospel of Thomas.

'The sisters and myself': In Jim Cotter's *Prayer at Night* (Cairns 1983) he refers to the 'Sisters of the Love of God' who by 'praying in the early hours of the morning … are aiming to make of the "day" and of the "night" a single whole Day.'

'Bread is broken' was written as a Communion song, and has been put to music by Nigel Walsh. Details of this and other Walsh-Skinner collaborations can be found on *nigelcwalsh.com*.

Invocations: these are companion pieces to the 40 Invocations previously published under that title (Wild Goose Publications, 2005). The first six here were written to accompany the installation of banners in St Stephen's Church, Exeter, following a major refurbishment programme. Of the others, 'O Lagoon' specifically refers to Bournda Lagoon in New South Wales, Australia, the water of which contains tea tree oil (an essential oil) from the nearby trees; and 'O Abba' was first published as a light-hearted addition to *Anthrop*, the Swedish translation of the original *Invocations* sequence.

Sources and acknowledgements

A number of the poems were first published in the previous poetry collections. 'Gospel psalm' was first published in *Green Christians*. 'Meditation on peace' was first published in a 'One World Week' resource pack.

'Probes' and 'Prayer meeting': both poems were inspired by the writings of R.S. Thomas.

I am very grateful to poet, fellow explorer and good friend Christopher South-gate for his comments on an early draft of *Utterly Staggering*.

Utterly Staggering was first published as a download, Wild Goose Publications, 2014

About the author

A Londoner by upbringing, Richard moved to Devon in 1975 to write a novel which remains as unpublishable now as it was then. Several collections of his poetry have, however, been published, including *Invocations* (WGP 2005). A former member of Cambridge University Footlights, he also occasionally writes and performs sketch-based comedy; and in recent years he has enjoyed a collaboration with composer Nigel Walsh, being the lyricist for their musical *Bethlehem!*, several liturgical pieces, and a number of songs. He and his wife are members of the Anglican parish of Central Exeter.